APPLAUSE FOR
THERE'S NO BUSINESS WITHOUT THE SHOW

"Becka gives a stunning performance in this book! It is unique, entertaining and effective as it provides you the trade secrets to give the sales performance of your life. Bravo!"

—DAVID COTTRELL
Best-selling author of *Monday Morning Leadership*
and *Monday Morning Choices*

"If you're in the sales game to make money and be a star, this is the book to read. This book puts the sizzle back into selling and will show you how to give the performance of your life."

—BILLY COX
Author of *The All-Star Sales Book*

"Tom Becka is known throughout talk radio as one of the most personable, entertaining and unique personalities on the air today. He successfully translates his star broadcasting qualities to the field of sales and marketing in this book, the result of which will be the emergence of scores of productive and happy account execs across the nation."

—MICHAEL HARRISON
Talkers Magazine

"This is one of the few times I didn't want a book to end. If you are in sales, this book will remind you why you get up in the morning.... a must-read for anyone who wants to be a success."

—VAN DEEB
Author of *Selling from the Heart*

"As an executive coach, I can see how this book is a powerful tool to cultivate success in business — from the sales department to the top salesperson — the CEO."

—DEBRA BENTON
Author of *How to Think Like a CEO* and *Executive Charisma*

"Tom knows how to be entertaining and he knows how to sell. This book is an easy read, yet heavy on information. This book will inspire, inform, entertain, and motivate you to achieve your full potential. Every day you have to get on that stage, and this book will show you how to make every performance an award winner. Buy this book before your competition does."

—MCGRAW MILHAVEN
KTRS Radio, St. Louis, MO

"I have toured with a range of musicians in a variety of genres. It doesn't matter whether it's an intimate club or a stadium with 70,000 people: Show business and sales are one and the same."

—CAROLYN SNELL
Tour manager for many national recording acts, Nashville, TN

"Tom Becka understands that in today's media-driven world, talent is not enough. When 'appearance means everything,' success in sales depends as much on promoting one's self as it does on promoting the product. You cannot just be a successful salesperson, you have to look and act like one. Tom's guidance follows sound psychological principles and, incorporated into sales practices, is likely to enhance any salesperson's efforts. As a bonus, Tom understands that humor is the balance for the stress inherent in a sales career."

—TERENCE W. BARRETT, Ph.D.
Licensed Psychologist, North Dakota State University

"Often sales professionals spend too much time focusing on process, methodology, and tools and forget that it's equally important to understand why buyers, their audiences, buy. Tom's book presents a fresh and unique approach—selling is really show business and gaining audience approval is paramount to success. Read this book to learn how and why the best sales professional must have a great deal in common with award-winning show business performers."

—BOB KANTIN
Founder and President, *SalesProposals.com*
Author of *Sales Proposals Kit for Dummies*
and *Why Johnny Can't Sell... And What to Do About It*

"My father was the best salesman I have ever known and a lot of what Tom is saying is the same wisdom my father taught me years ago. Everybody is in sales and everybody is in show business. This book would also be good for teachers, lawyers, or anyone who has to sell their ideas to others."

—DOUG STEPHAN
Host of the syndicated show
Doug Stephan's Good Day

"Tom has it spot on. The best thing about blending showmanship with salesmanship is that clients will actually enjoy dealing with you, even though you're after their money. Clients will be loyal, too, because it will be the rare salesperson who makes the impression you do."

—JOHN MAINELLI
National radio consultant and former program director WABC New York

"Sam Walton said, 'There is only one boss, the customer, and he or she can fire anybody in the company from the chairman on down by spending his or her money elsewhere.' Father Carroll Abbing said, 'The secret to happiness in life is to love and the essence of love is to serve.' Becka says to learn from the best people like these and become a great servant at serving your customer. Tom's book makes you want to improve yourself in becoming a better student, thus learning to become a better leader."

—JACK KAHL
Founder of Manco, Inc.
Internationally recognized speaker and author of *Leading from the Heart*

THERE'S NO
BUSINESS
WITHOUT THE

USING SHOWBIZ SKILLS
TO GET BLOCKBUSTER SALES

TOM BECKA

**ORPHEUM
BROTHERS
PRESS**

Omaha, Nebraska

LCCN: 2008926913
Library of Congress Cataloging information on file with publisher.

ISBN13: 978-0-9815461-0-0 (hardcover)
ISBN10: 0-9815461-0-2 (hardcover)

ISBN13: 978-0-9815461-1-7 (paperback)
ISBN10: 0-9815461-1-0 (paperback)

Orpheum Brothers Press
P. O. Box 31267
Omaha, Nebraska 68131
www.TomBecka.com

Editorial Services: Sandra Wendel
Book Design: Gary Withrow
Production and Marketing: Concierge Marketing Inc.

Printed in the United States of America
10 9 8 7 6 5 4 3 2 1

This book is dedicated to my Dad,
Raymond J. Becka, CLU.
A great salesman but a lousy singer.

CONTENTS

ACKNOWLEDGMENTS

Special thanks to my Mom, Joan, Michael, Renie, Tom, Andy, Michael Andrew, William, Matt, Jenny, Paul and Patty, McGraw, Katie, David C, Olivia, Giff, Gary, everyone at KFAB, The Dundee Dell, Jeff and Stacy, Bill, Dutch and Stacy, and Sarah.

A very special thanks to everyone who has told me no, tried to discourage me, or stand in my way. You've been great motivation and inspiration.

FOREWORD

As a stand-up comedian, Tom Becka spent his early days in the laugh industry driving down lonely, two-lane roads, hopping from one sleepy college campus to another. He'd wind up telling jokes to rowdy drunks in smoky small-town bars and paid his dues on the humor circuit by appearing in out-of-the-way supper clubs.

As a sales guy, Tom sold radio advertising, fertilizer, stereos, and even apple pies.

Tom realized—no matter the venue or the product—he was really selling himself. It was all about show business.

Eventually, Tom made it to the bigtime in both sales and stand-up. His stand-up comedy career took off. He headlined big-city clubs and opened for superstars. Then Tom parlayed his comedic work into a highly successful career as a talk radio host.

His influential radio show on KFAB in Omaha entertains tens of thousands of loyal listeners every weekday during the prime evening drive time. Together, Tom and I share a love for our surprisingly vibrant hometown of Omaha and a sense that the sales business is indeed the entertainment business.

The promo for Tom's radio show offers listeners a hearty dose of "honesty, integrity, and a sense of humor." That's Tom. This book offers the same smart talk.

Tom personifies the best of business and the best of sales. He combines them to create his own blend of talk and entertainment. He has an uncanny sense of curiosity, an unexpected sensitivity for the human condition, and a gift for saying the right things at the right time.

In this book, you'll find nuggets of insight you can use to be successful in your own world of sales. And you'll benefit from Tom's wit and wisdom. Most of all, you'll realize that sales and entertainment really are one and the same, with or without a microphone in your hand.

In this book, Tom shares his secrets to selling yourself because it's all about the show. Ladies and gentlemen, it's showtime!

—JEFF BEALS
Self Marketing Power: Branding Yourself as a Business of One

OVERTURE:

ANOTHER OPENING, ANOTHER SHOW

This is not your typical "how to" sales book. I won't just be focusing on basic fundamentals of sales principles. I assume that most people reading this book already have some experience and success in sales.

I won't be dealing with the "nuts and bolts" of a sales call. In fact many of the ideas that are going to be presented will fly in the face of some of the time-honored sales traditions. At times this book is going to challenge many of the beliefs of sales manager and salesperson alike.

But that's a good thing. If you don't challenge yourself, you don't grow.

Insanity is defined as doing the same thing repeatedly and expecting different results. Sales can be that way. You make a sales call and expect buyers to bite. They don't. You try it again. Still no bites. Something's wrong here. So what you are about to read is a cure for insanity.

There's No Business Without the Show is designed to be an idea starter. It's designed to get you thinking about sales in a different light. It's designed to motivate you, to inspire you, and to get you to question what you are doing and the way you are doing it.

If this book were a Hollywood movie, the preview would start with dramatic music and then the announcer would read in a big booming voice:

If you read only one book on sales this year, this is the book to read. In a world where the mundane is accepted, and the routine is routine, *There's No Business Without the Show* **dares to challenge the status quo. It dares to go where no other book on sales has gone before. Get on board now or be left behind. This is the start of the sales revolution.**

If I can get you to look at the sales process in a different light, you'll be a step ahead of your competition.

If you are new in the world of sales, you will benefit from this fresh approach. It will give you a perspective few beginning sales reps have. If you are a veteran, you will benefit from the insight these concepts provide.

In today's competitive world, everything is show business. For example, teachers can't teach without entertaining the class. Lawyers have to put on a show in front of a jury. Politicians are just as likely to get elected because they look good on TV and know how to inspire an audience than to win on their policies and platforms.

I believe that everything in life is show business, and that's what this book is about.

When performers go on stage, they have to convince the audience that they are the characters they are portraying. They have to sell their act to their customers—the audience. Is that really any different than what you do every day as a salesperson?

Every day you have to get before your audience. Many times you say the same things you said the day before. Just like the actor in a play or a stand-up comedian in a club has to repeat the same lines, yet make the act seem fresh, as if it's being said for the very first time.

When you go see a show, you not only give the performers your money, you give them something much more valuable. You give them your time. Can you imagine going to that performance and the actors just mechanically delivering their performance?

They may say every line as it's written, but without the passion, without the freshness, without the acting, you have wasted both your time and money.

With this book you will learn about standing out in a crowded field. You will learn about everything from overcoming stage fright to dealing with rejection to using props in your presentation, to coming back for the encore.

One of the problems with people who are in sales is that people think they are in sales. They're not in sales. They're in show business.

Let me repeat it one more time so it sinks in:

You are not in sales. You are in show business.

To get your message across, you have to be entertaining. You have to grab the attention of your audience, manipulate their emotions, leave a lasting impression, and get them to respond.

Your job is no different than that of an actor, a singer, a dancer, a comedian, a radio talk show host, or a mime.

You'll be amazed how much you can learn from successful Hollywood types.

When you deal with a customer (who from time to time will be referred to as your audience), there are times you have to act. There are times you have to tell jokes. There are times you have to be quiet. And yes there are even times when you have to do the old song and dance.

Are you prepared? You will be, once you have finished reading this book.

No matter what you are selling, your job is to make your audience (the customer) feel better. Your job is to leave that sales performance with the audience singing your song the way they do when they leave a Broadway musical.

You want your audience (again, your customer) to buy into what you are saying the way the ticket buyers bought in to Dustin Hoffman being an idiot savant in *Rainman*, or Tom Hanks portraying an astronaut, Meg Ryan's boyfriend, and later as a FedEx pilot stranded on a deserted island.

You want to stand out so that your audience will remember your name and want to see some of your other work. You don't want to be one of those actors who blends into the background. Those actors don't make any money. The stars that stand out do. And if you can stand out, and if you can be a star, you will find your sales, your market share, and your bank account growing.

You'll be amazed how much you can learn here from successful Hollywood types. This however is not going to be a book for aspiring thespians. This is a book for sales professionals to look at their craft in a new, exciting, and profitable light.

So enough with the fanfare. Dim the lights. Let's raise the curtain on Act One of your new life in sales.

ACT ONE
Image, Preparation, and Success

ACT ONE, SCENE ONE:

IMAGINE YOUR IMAGE

"I have gotten a lot more attention than ...
other women that I find incredibly beautiful.
And this has happened to me ever since
I was a girl, when I was flat, had no tooth,
was skinny and small as I could be. I always
got more attention than anyone else. If I
hadn't, I would have made sure I did."
—Actress Salma Hayek

The Screen Actors Guild represents over 120,000 working actors. How many can you name?

There are tens of thousands of Gold and Platinum records awarded to artists by the Recording Industry Association of America. How many come to mind?

There are thousands of television shows on network and cable stations. Do you know their names? For that matter how many of the cable networks can you list?

My point is that the entertainment field is very crowded. Just as competition in your field is very crowded. Yet some entertainers stand out from the crowd. Some performances are memorable. Some names are so recognizable that they become iconic.

Most do not.

Salma Hayek made sure people noticed her. Even when she was a skinny girl with no breasts or teeth, she was determined to be recognized. She was determined to be perceived as being special, even when she wasn't.

There are those who stand out from the crowd. Those whose names readily come to mind. How do they do it and what can we learn from them?

Whenever you think of any entertainer who is at the top of his or her field, a certain image comes to mind. For example, what do you see when you picture Justin Timberlake's dance moves or Ozzy Osbourne biting the head off bats? You see an image that works for the product they are trying to sell.

What does your audience think of when they think of you? How do you stand out in the crowd? What do you do to be memorable? What is your image? Can someone define you in just a few words?

I'm sure that you are a very complex and multifaceted person. But that doesn't matter to your audience. They want to be able to define you in a sentence or two.

- David Letterman, for example, is a late-night comedian from Indiana with a gap between his front teeth, and he wears light-colored socks with his loafers and double-breasted suits.
- Bruce Willis is an action movie star who's still friends with his ex-wife and her new, younger husband.
- Kenny Chesney is a country singer who was married for a few months to Renee Zellweger, the actress who gained weight to play a plump Bridget Jones.

Let's do a little exercise. I'm going to name a few genres in the entertainment field. You think of the first two celebrities that come to mind in that field. Then ask what makes them memorable.

For instance, if I said female romantic leading lady. You might think Sandra Bullock because she has a smart, sexy, girl-next-door appeal. Or Jennifer Aniston for her down-to-earth beauty. If I mentioned male rock star, Elvis or Mick Jagger might come to mind. Two entertainers with incredibly powerful images.

Now you try it. Think of the first two names that pop into your head. Don't dwell on one group too long.

Here are the categories:
- Male stand-up comic
- Female country singer
- Male TV star
- Female talk show host
- Politician

Did some names pop up automatically? What were the first images you thought of? Was it a favorable image?

Now think of two salespeople in your field besides yourself. Why did these names pop into your head? What made them stand out? Are they favorable reasons?

Now for the tough question:

What do people think of when they think of you?

Be honest. Is it favorable? Is it an image you want? Is it one that would pop out? Or would your audience have to think long and hard to come up with one?

In a moment, we'll come up with a few ways to enhance and capitalize on your image.

But first let's address the issue of the genres in which you couldn't think of a person in that field or you had great difficulty thinking of a person in that field.

If you couldn't think of someone, it may be because you have no interest in that field. If you don't like country music, you might not be able to name a female star. Or if you don't watch TV, you probably had to dig to think of a male star.

But in your lifetime you have listened to country and you have watched TV. Faith Hill and Jerry Seinfeld are doing just fine without you, even though you didn't name them. Just somehow nothing stood out for you. There was nothing you found appealing. That's all right. That's life.

My point is this: No matter how good you re, you're not going to be able to get everybody to listen and pay attention to you. You don't need everybody to be a success.

You just need as many of "your people" that you can get. Not everyone is going to be a fan. Don't worry about them. Focus on your audience. Then, once you've found your audience, superserve them to be a superstar.

BEFORE YOU CLOSE YOU NEED THE CLOTHES

Now let's build on that image. The first and the easiest way to build an image is with your clothing.

Would Willie Nelson have been able to cultivate his outlaw image if he wore a tuxedo? Would the Beatles have stood out if they didn't have their long hair? Would Pamela Anderson have the same image if she had worn clothes at all?

Clothing definitely says something about you. Yet most salespeople dress alike. Whether you are selling medical supplies, real estate, or high definition TVs at one of the big-box stores, the clothing that you wear is interchangeable with the clothing that other salespeople in your field are wearing.

And that uniform might help define you as A salesperson but how does it help define you as **THE** salesperson?

Stand out from the crowd. If you wear the same clothes every day, people will remember you. If you wear the exact same clothes every day, people will remember you but not in a good way (the smell will give you away).

Dress in a similar style. Wear something that blends in with what others in your field wear, yet stands out.

When I was on the road as a stand-up comic, I started out looking like every other stand-up comic from the era. As my act progressed, so did my sense of style. Okay, sense of style might be a slight hyperbole. Let's just say I learned to do some little things to stand out.

I not only wore the blue jeans with a sport coat like a lot of other stand-up comics, but I wore a slightly wrinkled shirt with the top button unbuttoned and a necktie slightly askew. To add to the image I added a nice fedora. Man, I was sharp.

It was a similar enough look for what people expected a comedian to look like, yet different enough from what the other comics were wearing.

With women it's much easier to create a style. For one thing, generally speaking, women think about clothes more than men do. Just walk through any mall in America and you will see countless stores catering to women's fashion. There are stores for formal wear, casual wear, professional women, and stay-at-home moms. There are stores for jewelry, handbags, and shoes.

The men get one store that sells dark suits and ties.

Regardless, it will be fairly easy to come up with something very unique. It won't have to be much, since the odds are your competition isn't doing anything at all. And when I say stand out, I don't mean like a sore thumb.

If your profession calls for conservative business attire, it's easy to be noticed if you show up in a bathing suit wearing nose plugs and flippers. That will make you unforgettable. It just won't make you many sales. (Don't ask how I know. Let's just say I found that out the hard way.)

But little accessories worn consistently will get you noticed and make you memorable.

If you are a woman, you can wear a certain piece of jewelry, a certain color outfit, or, if you are so inclined, maybe even hats. A man can consistently wear certain designer suits, a lapel pin, the same color tie, the same color shirt. Or, if you are so inclined, maybe even a hat.

If you wear eyeglasses, there are countless styles to choose from. Spend a little extra on frames and make them a pair people will remember. Make sure any style clothing you choose is age and status appropriate. But make it consistent. And when I say consistent, I mean wear the style every day.

It wouldn't be *Larry King Live* if Larry showed up one day and he wasn't wearing suspenders. Repetition builds success and makes you memorable. Wear the same thing differently every day.

Every night when David Letterman walks out on stage, he wears beige socks. He used to wear tennis shoes with his suits, but as he matured, his style changed. Yet his style is consistent.

Robin Williams used to wear bright suspenders every time he performed. He has evolved from that.

Elton John used to wear gaudy glasses and duck suits. While his style is more subdued these days, he still wears memorable eyewear, and his clothes still make an impression when he walks into a room.

Another way to be noticed is your hair. Just ask Donald Trump. Spend some money on your hair. If you're a woman, be contemporary, yet don't change your style or hair color every other day. If you're a man, go to the same stylist and be consistent with your cut.

There are a lot of real estate developers in New York City. But none of them has Donald Trump's hair. In fact, how many other New York real estate billionaire developers can you think of? Probably not many. Yet Donald Trump has used show business techniques to create a brand—a perceived value in the Trump name. With that perceived value in the Trump name, he can charge a lot more for his real estate.

When he makes a cold call to someone he wants to do business with, the call is returned because his reputation has preceded him. It's more than just Donald Trump's hair, but his hair has become one of his calling cards. It's been the butt of jokes, and "The Donald" has been laughing all the way to the bank.

Speaking of "The Donald," here's something else you might want to consider. Use a nickname. Bruce Springsteen is "The Boss." Jerry Lee Lewis is "The Killer." Rush Limbaugh is "El Rushbo."

A nickname can help with the image you are trying to project. It can also help make you a little more human, a little more endearing, and maybe even a person others can relate to. But a nickname isn't for everybody.

Don't try to force it or talk about yourself in the third person. Make it what other people are calling you. You can reinforce your nickname with your business cards, printed material, billboards, or just in your conversations.

For example, a killer real estate developer may bill herself as "the queen of condos." A car salesman might be "your luxury expert" or perhaps "the big man in sub-compacts."

Make your nickname strong, authoritative, successful, and one you can live with for a long time. Being known as the "whiz kid" might work when you are 22. But it might not have the same meaning when you are 55 with bladder problems.

There are other ways to project an image. Can you create a logo for your name on a business card that will stand out? The photo on the card is okay but it's overdone. What can you add to that to be memorable?

Do you like cars? Is your car special? Jay Leno has built quite a reputation for being a car lover. You don't need a warehouse filled with rare automobiles to have an image as a car buff.

I have a friend who is an avid hunter. He sells products that are geared towards men. That's important because a hunting image might not go over as well if he were selling cosmetics.

Although he doesn't go on his calls in camouflage, the trim on his briefcase is camouflaged. It's a subtle hint about what he likes to do on his off time. His best customers get homemade sausage and jerky.

Utilize what you have in your life and help make that your calling card. If you are a family person who enjoys going to your kids' Little League games, let your customers know. If you are a woodworker, perhaps you could have a few pictures of your work. A music lover might benefit from a specialty business card that plays a tune. If you are a gourmet chef, share a favorite recipe. Let your customers know. It helps build an image. It helps you stand out. It helps make you a success.

These are just a few ideas to get your brain started. I'm sure you can come up with a number of other suggestions that apply to your personality and your business.

Don't just blurt it out and spend more time talking about your hobbies than what you are there to sell. But by gently working it into the conversation, you will help create a favorable image.

Your customers can't spend money with you if they don't think of you. Stand out and you'll be the first person they think of when it's time to buy. Stand out and they'll look forward to your visits rather than being bothered by another salesperson. Stand out and you are on your way to success.

YOU CAN BE AN OVERNIGHT SUCCESS,
But It's Going to Be a VERY Long Night

"Desperation is the perfume of the young actor. It's so satisfying to have gotten rid of it. If you keep smelling it, it can drive you crazy."

—Actress Uma Thurman

THE PERFORMER'S ATTITUDE

B eing a successful entertainer has as much to do with attitude as it does with talent. After all, as the old song in the play Damn Yankees goes, "You gotta have heart."

Jerry Seinfeld says that being a comedian is a lot like being a mass murderer. No matter how many times someone tries to talk you out of it, you are still going to do it.

The same is true for successful salespeople. No matter how many times people tell you no, or try to prevent you from being a success, you are going to keep on. Even if the person trying to hold you back is you.

One of the biggest enemies any performer has—whether they be a star of stage, screen, or sales—is themself. To be a star you have to take risks. You have to take chances. You have to go ahead and do it, even if the odds are long. After all, the greater the risk, the greater the reward.

There is no such thing as an overnight success. That's true in all aspects of life, but it's especially true in show business and in sales. How many auditions does someone have to go on before they are hired for a job? How many times have they heard, "Next," at the cattle call? How many times have they been rejected? Turned down? Humiliated? Misled? Lied to? Passed over?

Yet the successful stars don't let it get to them. They put a smile on their face, set their egos aside, and try again. And again. And again.

My first job in radio was working overnights at a small radio station in Green River, Wyoming. As the old joke goes, Green River is not the end of the world, but you can see it from there. Now, you don't work overnights in a small Wyoming town if people in the industry think you have a bright future ahead of you. It was the only job I could get. I didn't care. I was in show business making $600 a month and loving every minute of it.

Well, almost every minute of it. There were times when I was working at 3 a.m. in the middle of a cold Wyoming winter when I wondered what in the hell I was doing. There were times when the people around me suggested that I should give it all up and do something else.

There are going to be times when you are possessed with self doubt. That's only normal.

All successful entertainers have had those times when they weren't sure that they could make it. Or, if they had some success, weren't sure if they could take it to the next level. But deep down inside was something that made them go on.

Remember, if the goal is really worthwhile, it's not going to be easy. Deep down, every successful star knew that failure was not an option. Deep down, they knew that success was going to be theirs. Every obstacle they overcame just made them one step closer to the top.

Denial isn't always such a bad thing.

Darrell Hammond from *Saturday Night Live* fame told me that when producer Lorne Michaels gave him the call to tell him that he had the job, Darrell had to brush off the cockroaches crawling on the phone handset. At the time, he was crashing on a friend's couch. Things were not going as well as he had wanted. He had had some success as a stand-up comic, but at the time he got his big break, he was just trying to get by.

Darrell had been in show business a long time working the comedy clubs around the country. Even when things looked bleak, deep down he knew he had talent. He knew he had what it takes, and even if people were trying to talk him out of a career in comedy, he knew he was still going to do it.

Darrell now holds the record as the longest running cast member in the history of *Saturday Night Live*. He has even performed before President Clinton as President Clinton. He has been in movies, had his own stand-up special, and headlined theaters across the country. He no longer has to sleep on a friend's couch with cockroaches doing their best to convince him he should give up on his dreams.

For years I was a successful radio salesperson and sales manager. But one day I went on stage at a local comedy club to try an open-mic night. I was only going to do it one time just to say that I did it. I knew it would help create an image with my customers.

I got some laughs, and the manager suggested that I continue to come back. The next thing you know, people wanted to hire me to work their clubs.

I quit my successful radio sales job with health benefits and a 401k and went on the road with no guarantees and little money. I didn't have much, but I had dreams, I had ambition, and I had a positive attitude.

Your attitude is everything. There was a time early in my stand-up career when I was so broke that I spent months living in a $100-a-week flophouse in Atlanta. It was a small step up from sleeping in my car. I would sleep with a chair propped against the door for extra security against the transients, the drug dealers, and the prostitutes that were also living there.

To get me through this down time in my life, I would convince myself that all of this will look good in the autobiography. I would joke that I was living the life of a jazz musician. And to be honest I was in a bit of denial about my current surroundings.

But denial isn't always such a bad thing.

By being in denial I didn't focus on my current life situation. I didn't let it get me down. I knew better things were on the horizon for me. I knew that this was just part of the process to pay my dues to achieve what I wanted out of life.

And I was right.

I could have let my surroundings get the best of me. I had plenty of opportunities to give up. I could have fallen prey to my environment and become "one of them"— one of the other residents who had given up on their dreams, if they ever had any dreams to give up on in the first place.

But I wouldn't let that happen. And neither should you. Attitude is everything.

It's not easy to be a successful salesperson. You've got to pay your dues. Paying your dues is not easy. But the rewards are more than worth it.

ACT ONE, SCENE THREE:

YOU WERE GOING TO GET YOUR BIG BREAK
the Day After You Quit

What a great old showbiz adage: "You were going to get your big break the day after you gave up." It shows that you never know when you might get that chance of a lifetime. But one thing's for sure, it's not coming after you retire.

You could even modify that a little and say, "You were going to get your big sale the day after you quit." Nothing pays off like perseverance. Just like Jerry Seinfeld's quote about a comic being like a mass murderer. You have got to want it.

To be a success in stand-up, you have to be driven, you have to be dedicated, and you have to persevere. The same is true with sales. And it's much easier to be dedicated to a life in sales than it is to be dedicated to a life in show business.

When I started my stand-up career, there were times I had to sleep in my car. I stayed in motels that were such dumps I had to sleep on top of the sheets, and I refused to use the showers because of the mold.

I had to play every dump in America. I played in a college cafeteria during lunchtime, a bar in Topeka where my stage was a coffee table, and a Christmas party for the staff at an all-you-can-eat pizza joint.

What made the Christmas party so memorable was that while I was trying to do my routine, the kids of the staff were running around, playing video games and skee ball. And to make matters worse, most of the restaurant's employees were illegal immigrants who didn't speak English.

Speaking English may not be necessary to wash dishes, but it is kind of a prerequisite for enjoying an American stand-up performance.

While each of these shows was devastating at the time, they all taught me a valuable lesson, and they were all a part of paying my dues. I'll bet it was easier for you starting out in sales.

You get into doing stand-up comedy with dreams of having your own sitcom, but you start out telling jokes to college kids in a lunchtime cafeteria while they study for their next class and get another order of fries. Before you hold down the 8:30 prime time slot for the networks, you've got to hold down the biscuits and gravy from some truck stop diner on a forgotten highway in the middle of nowhere.

That's really not any different than getting into sales. The person who hires you tells you that you can make a high six-figure income. Then they give you the worst leads, the worst hours, and the worst support imaginable.

Basically they send you out there to see how badly you want it, to see how badly you are going to work for it, and to see if you have the stuff to be able to handle success when it eventually comes by handling the failure that happens early on in a sales career.

The good news is that in sales you can still make a living doing your craft while working your way to the top. In show business you've got to really pay your dues and take a lot of lousy jobs while trying to make it big in your chosen field.

- Demi Moore was a debt collector.
- Stephen King got the inspiration for writing *Carrie* while a janitor in a girls locker room.
- Warren Beatty caught rats.

At least you are paying your dues selling your product or service. It's a lot better than catching rats.

So how do you keep your head up and your spirits up during the dark days of sales? By being in denial—at least a little bit in denial.

You may know that you have a lousy sales list. And you may know that the economy is slow. And you may know that you are a new salesperson. And you may know that it's going to be a tough sale. But remember what Albert Einstein, world-renowned vaudeville comedian, said, "Imagination is more important than knowledge."

So imagine the opposite. Use your imagination to see into the future when you are making the sale. Use your imagination to picture yourself as your company's number one sales leader. Use your imagination to visualize buying your boat or vacation home. Use your imagination to make your dreams happen.

Being a successful salesperson isn't easy. You have to pay your dues. But once your dues are paid, you can live a great life as a sales superstar. You can enjoy a profitable career and look back fondly at the "good old days" when you were just starting out and playing to a college crowd at lunchtime.

After all, the best stories are those you tell about when you were just starting out and working your way to success. They are the stories that will inspire others. They are the stories everyone wants to hear.

☆

ACT ONE, SCENE FOUR:

STAGE FRIGHT
Nature's Way of Telling You You're Alive

S tage fright is nothing new. Many great performers have had to deal with it over the years. Legend has it that John Lennon threw up almost every night before going on stage.

Many entertainers are shy in their personal lives. David Letterman, Brad Pitt, and Carrie Underwood are all known to be shy and very protective of their time away from performing. Many great performers suffer from stage fright. But they have all been able to overcome their shyness and fears to become international superstars.

How about you?

We are taught when we are young to never talk to strangers. Yet when you become a salesperson, that's exactly what you are supposed to do. You are supposed to forget what your mother told you all those years ago, and you are supposed to start talking to strangers.

It's not uncommon for even experienced salespeople to get nervous before a cold call on a prospective client. In fact it's normal and can be used as a good thing if you don't let the fear of the unknown take control and prevent you from making the presentation.

Take the fear, the nerves, the stage fright, and make it work for you. Fear makes you focus. Fear makes you aware of your surroundings. Fear gives you an adrenalin rush. And all of these can benefit you in a sales performance.

The first thing to remember about stage fright is that it's perfectly normal and that you aren't some kind of freak if you get the butterflies before a big pitch. Many of your co-workers and competitors are going through the same thing, but nobody wants to admit it or talk about it. Nobody wants to admit they are scared.

But if others are going through the same thing, what are you worried about? The main thing to remember is best summed up by an old television ad for a deodorant: "Never let them see you sweat."

Overcoming the fear and anxiety that many people face before a sales call may be as simple as realizing it's natural and that others are battling the same fears. And as we all know, there's comfort in knowing you are not alone.

To relax, you can take deep breaths. Breathe in through the nose and out through the mouth. You can imagine pleasant thoughts, listen to relaxing music, or, if you're in a bit of a hippie mood, burn incense.

Take the time while you are deep breathing to focus on the sales call. Imagine what it is going to be like.

Most great entertainers visualize what the performance is going to be like before they ever take the stage. They imagine the audience. They imagine how they will react to every word they say and every move they make. Before the curtain rises, they use their mind's eye to see the lights, smell the smells, and visualize the final results. They envision the standing ovation long before it happens.

You should do the same.

Take a moment to visualize the sales call. Imagine how your customer will react to every word you say and every move you make. Before you make your pitch, use your mind's eye to see the client, their business, imagine what will go right and what might go wrong.

And while you are playing out the performance in your mind, prepare your adlibs to handle any situation. That's right. Prepare your adlibs. In the entertainment field adlibs are very rarely as off-the-cuff as they may seem.

As a comic when I was on stage and someone would walk into the showroom while the show was in progress, I would stop the routine I was doing and welcome the person to the show. Then I would ask them if there was anything I could get them—like a watch.

Do you know that most comedians have their heckle lines already prepared? A heckle line is the response a comedian gives when someone in the audience starts to hassle the comics when they're on stage. By preparing the heckle lines, they know just the right thing to say to quiet the hecklers and put them in their place before the loud, drunken audience members can ruin the performance.

With a heckler, a new comedian might use a variation of the tried-and-true putdown, "Hey, buddy, I don't go to the [insert name of minimum wage job here] and bother you when you're working." Even if a savvy audience has heard the line before, it always gets a laugh.

Johnny Carson said adlibbing is misunderstood. He said that it's not coming up with a fresh, original line every time but rather adlibbing is recall. It's about remembering a line and using it when the situation is right. It's about taking an old punch line and modifying it to the current situation. An adlib often comes from envisioning what might be said and then being ready for it.

You should do the same thing.

Prepare your responses in advance to any objections or disruptions you might face. Then rehearse saying them so they sound natural and spontaneous. If they sound like a canned response, you will lose your credibility. Make sure they sound as if it's the first time you've ever said that. Make it sound like you just thought of the response.

Sometimes an adlib will be genuine. The client will say something, and your preparation gives you the confidence to speak off-the-cuff. To go off script, if you will. When those adlibs work, remember them. They'll come in handy at a future date.

Adlibs are generally used to overcome objections. If you can make the client laugh, or just smile, with your adlib, you've won half the battle. Keep all of your adlibs in the back of your mind. If you don't need a certain phrase or thought for today's sales performance, you'll be able to use it in the future.

Use your feelings of fear before the show to prepare and gain confidence so that you don't end up with the look of panic on your face if something goes wrong during the performance.

Do you see how preparing your adlibs will help you overcome stage fright? By being overly prepared, you'll be more sure of yourself, and that confidence will shine through and belie any sense of fear you had prior to the performance.

You can also use stage fright as an occasion to focus. Face the fears. What's the worst that could happen? What's the best? If you visualize these situations when you are preparing for the show, you will be amazed at how much better it will go.

Even if you don't suffer from stage fright, it's best to take some time before any sales presentation to focus.

We are taught when we are young to never talk to strangers.

On Broadway the actors might do a play hundreds and in some cases thousands of times. Yet before every show, they take time to close their eyes and get ready. In their mind they see themselves on the stage, nailing their lines, hitting all the notes of their songs, and signing autographs after the show.

How many salespeople actually do this? How many times do they just go through the motions without even thinking about what they are saying? They are just doing their lines— the same lines they have done a million times before.

Just because an actor has said the lines a million times before is irrelevant. It's the first time the audience has heard them. The same is true with you.

Make sure you deliver your lines with a fresh approach every time you deliver the sales pitch. It seems so elementary but it's true. You may have made the same sales pitch hundreds times. You can recite the benefits of your product in your sleep. The sales pitch may be old hat to you, but it's the first time the client has heard it. Don't just regurgitate what you've said countless times before. Make it seem as if this is all brand new and the client is the only person to whom you've made these points.

Putting it back in the show business realm, make every performance as fresh as the first performance. Can you imagine spending big bucks on tickets to a Broadway play like *Cats* or *Jersey Boys* and the actors just mumble the lines or deliver them half-heartedly because they've said those lines so many times before? You'd feel ripped off. You'd be angry. You'd bad-mouth the show to all of your friends.

Don't let that happen to your sales presentation.

To overcome stage fright or sales reluctance

- Be prepared but not too familiar.
- Be focused but not to the point that you ignore your surroundings.
- Be relaxed but not too comfortable.
- Be energized but not manic.
- Be scripted but seem spontaneous.

You'll leave the stage a big success with rave reviews.

ACT TWO
Ready, Set, Rehearse

ACT TWO, SCENE ONE:

YOU DON'T HAVE TO BE A STAR
to Be in This Show

Y ou don't have to really be in show business to get a feel for what it's like to be on stage. Here are a couple of ideas to get you comfortable about the concept of using show business techniques for a sales presentation.

Do one or all of these to get out of your comfort zone. Push the envelope. Try new things. Once you have attempted and succeeded at these, you'll find it so much easier to be able to implement the ideas I present in this book.

IDEA 1: AUDITION FOR A PART IN A PLAYHOUSE PRODUCTION.

Call your local playhouse and find out when the next auditions will be held. It doesn't matter what the play is going to be. You may be surprised. You just might get a part. Even if you don't, just auditioning will help your sales delivery in a number of ways.

When actors go on an audition, they are doing the ultimate sales job. They have got to sell themselves to the producer and director. Go on the audition and make sure they notice you.

In an audition you may not know what character you are going to be reading for in advance. They will hand you a script and tell you to go. You've got to become that person on a moment's notice. You've got to instantly adapt.

And if you get the part, you'll learn even more.

Remember when I said you have to make every sales pitch seem like it's being said for the first time? Well, during rehearsals, you'll learn to say the same things over and over again while making it sound as if you are saying them for the first time. You'll practice keeping your performance fresh. You'll learn to take other people's words and make them your own.

When you are working with other actors, it forces you to listen to what they are saying before you respond. If you've been successful in sales for any length of time, you know that listening is just as important, if not more so, than talking in a sales presentation.

You will understand how the show must always go on. You can't let negativity in your personal life show up when you are on stage. It doesn't matter if you've just had a fight with your spouse, or if the mechanic tells you your car can't be repaired. When it's showtime, you are another person, and the audience doesn't care what's going on in your real life.

The same is true when you are making a sales call, but you'd be surprised how many salespeople let their personal problems affect their sales presentations.

Being an actor in a play forces you to work with others. It helps you understand that you have to depend on other people to be a success. Many salespeople tend to be too self-centered. They don't realize that there are many others who are a part of their success.

Often in the real world, salespeople will take the support staff or the people in charge of the product for granted. To be a successful salesperson and to guarantee customer satisfaction, you have to work as a team.

The best actor in the world is a flop if the stagehands, the musical director, and the ticket sellers aren't there to support them. Appreciate the people who enable your success.

IDEA 2: PREPARE A FIVE-MINUTE ROUTINE FOR OPEN-MIC NIGHT AT THE LOCAL COMEDY CLUB.

Five minutes might not seem like a long time, but in the world of stand-up comedy, it can be an eternity. It could very well be the single most frightening thing you will ever do. It can also be the single most exciting and invigorating thing you will ever do.

Prepare five minutes of completely original jokes. Write them yourself. Don't steal from other comedians. Write about your experiences. Write about your family, your life, your job. Put together a little routine and then get ready to perform it at an open-mic night.

There's a good chance you will bomb. But that's okay. By doing the stand-up itself, you will accomplish many things.

- You will overcome fear.
  This will help you be fearless when you are asking for a big buy or facing a mean, unfriendly client.
- You will have to deal with rejection.
  You'll find that after dealing with the rejection of a comedy crowd, dealing with Bob in purchasing won't be so daunting.

Doing stand-up will help you write to get your ideas across in an edited, succinct manner.

"We're [comedians] always selling ...
We're always trying to convince or persuade
somewhat ... Timing is very important."
—Comedian George Carlin

To be successful in stand-up, you have to get the audience to like you. You have to get strangers to feel good about what you have to say. You have to get in front of people who don't have a clue who you are and make them believe that you have something important they need to hear. And they have to do it from the moment you walk out on stage.

Walk on that stage with an attitude. The attitude that you are funny and the audience is going to laugh. Don't be cocky but be confident.

Be the right kind of confident. NBA coach Phil Jackson (Hey, sports is the entertainment industry.) has told his players, "Confidence carried the right way is great. Confidence carried over the edge is arrogance."

Genuine laughter is an involuntary reaction. When you get someone to laugh, you get them to do something that they might not normally do. You are getting them to do what you want them to do. You are manipulating their emotions. In their own way you are getting them to say yes to what you are saying.

Do you see how that might relate to a sales call?

After you have your five minutes of material prepared, edit it down to your best three minutes. It's always better to leave them wanting more.

"You can't have too much confidence in comedy. The more you have, the more you can use."

—Comedian Jerry Seinfeld

IDEA 3: ONE NIGHT, WHEN YOU AREN'T DRUNK, GO SING KARAOKE.

Most people wouldn't even think about singing karaoke unless they were totally hammered. After all, most people don't like their voices. Most people don't like getting up before big crowds. Most people are cowards.

But singing karaoke benefits you much the same way that doing stand-up does. You learn stage presence. You learn how to sell a song. You work on delivering to an audience and grabbing their attention.

Have you ever been to a karaoke bar? When the average singer gets up there and goes through the motions, you can see the audience lose interest. The crowd starts to ignore the singer and they talk to the people next to them. They get up to go to the bathroom. They see what's on the television over the bar.

But a karaoke singer who knows how to sell a song (they don't even have to be the best singer, just know how to sell it) can capture the audience's attention and have them hang on every note.

People who know what they are doing can get up on stage and take charge. They take command. They let you know that they mean business.

Learn how to capture a karaoke audience's attention, and it will be easier to capture the attention of a client. But do it when you are sober. Don't wait until you've got a few drinks in you and your friends are forcing you on stage. Do it with a clear head and the definite intention of getting on that stage and selling that song.

After you have learned to capture their attention, you can belly up to the bar to your heart's content. You deserve it.

IDEA 4: STUDY WHAT GREAT PERFORMERS DO.

The next time you watch a play, listen to a singer sing, or go to the movies, study what the great performers are doing. What are they doing in their shows that you can use in your presentations? You'll be surprised how much there is. After all, every great performer has sold you on their talents.

If you believe that John Travolta is really a woman singing and dancing in *Hairspray*, you've been sold. If you believe that Larry really is a cable guy, you've been sold. If you believe that when you go to Cheers, everybody really does know your name, you've been sold.

Watch what great performers do and ask yourself a simple question: How would that work in a sales performance?

NOW IT'S TIME TO TAKE YOUR ACT ON THE ROAD.

After you have done the stand up, or the acting, or the karaoke, you can work it into the casual conversations you have with your clients, which will help them remember you even more. You'll stand out from the other sales reps because you'll be "the one who tried stand-up" or "their singing salesperson." Remember you've got to put images in their heads that make you unforgettable.

Your city has hundreds of civic groups that want and need guest speakers for their breakfasts, lunches, and dinners. Many of these club members want and need what you have to offer.

Why not put together a speech about what you do and how it can benefit them?

I'm not talking about a full-blown sales presentation in front of the Rotary Club. I'm talking about a speech discussing how your product or service is fitting into today's changing world and how your product or service can make people's lives a little better.

If you are in financial sales, talk about saving for retirement. If you are in automobile sales, talk about changing consumer trends. If you are in clothing sales, do a speech on fashion.

Make it generic. Make it compelling. Make it entertaining and humorous. Make it about them. But, most important, make it easy for them to get in touch with you if they have any questions, or if they see the need to buy what you are selling.

These extracurricular activities will benefit you in your sales career at the same time by doing something a little different, it will help you take your mind off your sales career. After all, you know what they say about all work and no play.

To be a successful salesperson, first and foremost, you've got to be a successful person. These hobbies will benefit you in your professional life, but they are fun too. You'll meet a lot of interesting people. Some of whom may become customers.

ACT TWO, SCENE TWO:

FIND A NICHE

"I do what I do because I love it. I am at peace with it and I have found my niche."
—Actress Loretta Swit

Every successful entertainer is known for one or maybe two things. They are an actor. A singer. A sportscaster. A comedian. A supermodel. Sometimes they are a hyphen, as in singer-songwriter or actor-director. But very rarely do you find one who has had much success branching outside their niche.

Oh, sure, you get the occasional Barbra Streisand who parlays her singing career into an acting, directing, producing, and political career. But most successful performers have the thing they are known for and stick with that.

Bob Denver played Gilligan on television. He was a comedic actor and would never have been taken seriously as a romantic lead. On the other hand, Brad Pitt would have a hard time making anyone believe that he was stranded on a desert island as the Skipper's "little buddy." Each has a niche. So much so that oftentimes a casting director will ask for a "Josh Hartnett or a Jack Nicholson type."

Now let's transfer that to what you do.

- What is your niche in sales?
- What are you known for?
- What is your type?
- Are you a problem solver? An idea person? A hard closer?

And perhaps the most important question: What can you do that nobody else is doing?

Most salespeople are just salespeople. They do their job. They make their calls. But what about finding your niche?

Take a look at what you are selling and ask yourself who are the customers that you can superserve. Now I don't necessarily mean what clients are the biggest or who have the most money, but who can you superserve?

I have known many advertising salespeople over the years who have taken a small local account and paid so much attention to them that they became a large regional or even national account. They did this by becoming a small business advertising specialist. They took the smaller accounts with more potential and worked with them to solve their advertising problems. They would find businesses that had a lot of potential and gradually built them up so they had a lot of money to spend.

While everybody else was busy fighting over the bigger advertising accounts and getting a small percentage of the big boys' budgets, these savvy salespeople would focus on the smaller accounts and get most or all of their budget. They had ideas for accounts the big advertising agencies would shun. They became the problem solvers for a specific type of advertiser, and by the time these accounts became big enough for the agencies to take notice and try to steal, the sales superstars were so entrenched that the advertisers wouldn't even think of leaving them.

To form a niche it's good to zig when everybody else is zagging. I know it seems impossible now, but there was a time when Oprah was just another host in the sea of daytime talk programs. She was competing against Jerry Springer, Phil Donahue, Sally Jessy, Maury Povich, and others.

Most of the other programs were going for the sensational topics such as strippers, incest, cheating spouses, and so on. Oprah made a point of saying that she would not be a part of this trend, that she would not do programs on bisexual wife-swapping dwarfs. Oprah was going to focus only on life-reaffirming topics. Topics that would inspire, bring hope, and change people's lives.

She, in effect, became the anti-Springer and it paid off big for her. She found the niche that wasn't being served by most of the other shows on the air at the time. She refused to follow the trend. She also didn't take the low road, which is often the easier road to take. She took the more difficult high road. She zigged while everyone else was zagging.

Now this came with a considerable risk.

TV stations and advertisers like the easy money. They like copycat programs. They see what everyone else is selling and put out more of the same. Oprah didn't like it. She saw an audience that wasn't being served and she served it. She was also true to her own values. Her show would not have been as big a success if she had made those changes just for the money. She changed the direction of her show because that was her niche. That was who she is.

To form a niche, it's good to zig when everybody else is zagging.

Now what about you?

Your sales managers are most likely pointing you in a certain direction because that's what sells. Most managers don't encourage taking risks. Most don't promote thinking outside the box. They want results and they want it now.

Creating your niche can take some time, and you may have to continue doing things the old way while you gradually become the niche expert.

Ask yourself these questions (be honest):

- What are my strongest points as a salesperson?
- Then take those points and ask how can I make them stronger? How can I accentuate them?
- How can I take these strong points and have them be my calling card?

Getting back to Oprah. She is obviously a passionate and caring person. She took those traits in her personality and fine-tuned them to create an image, a niche, an empire.

So what are your strong points? How can you use them to create an image? To create a niche? To create an empire?

Then the tougher questions need to be asked. What are your weakest points as a salesperson? Are these flaws important enough to work to make them stronger? Or are they something you can just minimize and hide?

For example, if one of your weak points is that you are awful with paperwork, you are going to have to work to make that better or hire someone to do that for you. The attention to detail is very important to being a sales superstar.

If, on the other hand, your weak point is that you drive a messy car, you have three options:

1. Obviously you can clean your car.
2. You park far enough away so your clients never have to see your car.
3. You make the messy car become part of your legend. You can be known as the salesperson who doesn't have time to clean his car because he's always too busy with his or her customers.

Now, you do have to make sure you pay extra attention to your clients; otherwise, you'll be known as the sloppy-pig-who-is-so-unorganized-nothing-gets-done-right salesperson. But if everything else is good, the car could become your calling card. In other words, if possible, find a way to make the negatives into positives.

- Tom Cruise is short.
- Ray Charles was blind.
- Oprah was fat, then skinny, then fat, now average.

All have taken these perceived negatives and turned them into positives. These perceived weak points weren't really negatives after all.

I cannot stress this enough: If the rest of the product wasn't there, these other flaws could have been fatal. It's not like the entertainment world is clamoring for a short guy who can't act, or a blind piano player who hits all the wrong notes.

But if the service is there, the product is there. The attitude and delivery are there. You can take a negative and make it part of your niche.

So ask yourself what your niche is. Ask yourself what niche isn't being served. Ask yourself what niche can be better served.

Then be known as being that expert who handles those problems and offers the solutions. Be known as the salesperson who knows the product better than anyone else. Be known as the salesperson you can reach anytime day or night. Be known as the salesperson who is the king or queen of the niche.

IT SEEMS IMPOSSIBLE
But People Buy Stuff
They Don't Like, Want, or Need

No matter what you are selling, you have a preconceived notion of who your clientele are. Perhaps these come from experience. Perhaps your sales manager told you the types you'll deal with. Perhaps it's just a gut feeling.

And while these reasons may be true for your core customer, every day, people who wouldn't normally buy a certain product or service are going against the conventional wisdom and buying things no one ever thought they would. The entertainment industry is proof of that.

From my own experience I can tell you that people buy against the stereotypes all the time. For instance, I don't like rap music, but look at my iPod and you'll find songs by

Eminem, Will Smith, and Sir Mix-A-Lot. I don't like bloody slasher movies, but I've spent money for tickets to see *The Texas Chainsaw Massacre* and its remake.

I have no need for Lindsay Lohan, but I bought my niece a copy of *Freaky Friday*, and I bought tickets to see Lindsay in *A Prairie Home Companion*.

Now I will grant you I am not a heavy user of these talents and I am not their target consumer, but I have still spent my hard-earned money on something they were selling.

Now convert that to your own field. How many times have you dismissed a potential customer just because the person didn't fit the mold? You automatically assume that because of the way he or she was dressed, past buying habits, or your past experiences that it's not worth your time.

Over the extent of your sales career, how many thousands of dollars have you left on the table? Ten of thousands? Hundreds of thousands? Millions? To capture this money, you'll need to expand your vision and you need to tell a better story.

Expand your vision to include the tertiary markets for your product. No matter what you are selling, there are untapped markets you can reach. Now you need to expand your story to reach these markets. It's all about "The Story."

Take any blockbuster movie. *Star Wars*, for example, could have been nothing more than a big budget, special effects movie where teenaged boys would flock to the theaters to see cool intergalactic battles in which spaceships got blown up. Or *Titanic* could have been nothing more than a big ship hitting an even bigger ice cube. But both of these stories and countless other successful movies, plays, and TV shows expanded their plot lines to hit a broader, secondary market.

Yes, *Star Wars* is more than light sabres. It's a story about family, about life and death, and conflict. It's a story that resonates with the human spirit. They just surround this story with computer-generated special effects, Dolby 5.1 sound, and a galaxy far far away.

It could be argued that James Cameron put his romantic love story on a sinking ship just so he could interest men in seeing the classic story of someone falling in love when they are betrothed to someone else. The sinking ship and its special effects got the younger male demographic interested in a movie they might not have cared for in another setting. Thus making *Titanic* the largest grossing movie of all time.

You should do the same. Telling a good story sells things.

To capture this money, you need to expand your vision, and you need to tell a better story.

Now take a look at whatever it is you are selling. Are there expanded markets you could be reaching? How do you go about it?

First put yourself in the place of the audience. What do they need? What do they want? What do they need and want that they are unaware that they need and want?

Now take your product or service and start to expand how it can fill those needs and wants, both known and unknown. : Take the pickup truck industry, for instance. For years only farmers and ranchers drove pickups. Then the car industry got wise. They expanded their story to tell people in urban settings that they too needed and wanted pickup trucks. They cleverly sold the idea of ruggedness and the great outdoors to a bunch of lawyers who spend all day sitting behind a desk.

They then took the pickup truck concept and modified it to reach the soccer moms, and, voila, the minivan was born. The minivan is really just a pickup truck for moms and kids.

So think outside the box. Is there a way you can modify your product or service to reach an entirely different and new demographic? Listen to your family and friends. They may tell you how to do it without them really telling you how to do it. Go to people you would not think of as your customer for your product and ask them what it would take to get them to buy it.

It may take a number of interviews, but somewhere in there someone will tell you something that will make a light go off and will help you generate a new market.

Don't limit yourself. Sell to people your competition is ignoring. Tell a good story. Then watch your income rise.

SELL IT, BABY ... SELL IT!

Before a comedian can try a new joke on the audience, he has to believe that it's funny. If he doesn't think it's funny, the odds are the audience won't think it's funny.

Even if it is.

Before a singer can make you believe her heart is broken, she has to feel it in the song. Before actors can make you believe they really are the characters, they have to completely understand the persona of the roles they are playing.

They have to get inside their characters' motives, their emotions, their history. They have to believe they are the character before they can make you believe they are the character.

Are you doing that with your sales presentation? Do you really believe in the product or service? Do you totally understand all of its benefits and features? Are you convinced that what you are telling the customer is really true? Or are you just reading a script?

If you truly believe what you are saying, you can sell it with enthusiasm. You can sell it with conviction and emotion. If you don't believe it, then you need to take some time and do some soul searching. If you don't believe in the product or service you are selling, ask yourself why. Find out what it is about what you are selling that you can't get excited about. Then ask if this is a genuine reason or if it's just an excuse for failure.

If you can't reconcile what keeps you from having total belief in what you are selling, then you need to search for the product or service you can totally believe in.

Think of what you are selling the way a Hollywood star thinks about taking a role.

If Hollywood stars take a part that they don't believe is right for them, they run the risk of having a bad performance. A bad performance can ruin a career. A bad performance can seriously limit the amount of money they can command on their next movie. And a bad performance can make them the laughingstock of the nation. Just ask Ben Affleck about making bad choices.

The same is true for the sales superstar. Just because you may not be totally sold on what you are selling doesn't mean it's a bad product. It just means that it's not right for you. You need to get into what you are selling the way an actor gets into a character. You need to understand all the advantages and disadvantages of your product or services. You need to believe in your product 110 percent.

When I do stand-up comedy, there is always pressure when trying out a new joke. If I don't believe it's funny, then the audience probably won't believe it's funny. Sure, sometimes you might get a laugh here or there with a joke you don't believe in, but, for the most part, if I don't believe it will get a laugh, it won't.

On the other hand, there have been jokes that I think are funny that might not work for any other comic. But I believe in it and I sell it to get a laugh.

Actors will constantly turn down parts because they are not right for the part. You should do the same when you decide what you want to sell. Don't just take a sales job for the sake of taking a sales job. Find the product you believe in. If there aren't any openings there, sell yourself and make them hire you.

Work to get the job you want. Performers are constantly selling themselves to get the jobs they want. You should do the same. Find whatever it is that you want to sell and sell it, baby, sell it!

BUILD A FAN BASE

Do you have a fan club? I'm not talking about a supportive spouse or family members. Although that kind of fan club is incredibly important. I mean a real life fan club made up of members who think of you as the go-to person whenever they need your goods or services.

A fan club of loyal customers might feel as if they are part of your team, and you are part of their team. A fan club is more than just a satisfied customer base.

You probably don't have a fan club, but great performers do. And you should too.

Now I don't mean you should have a fan club where you send your customers autographed pictures and super-hero decoder rings. But a fan base where you keep your customers up-to-date on the latest developments in your products or services. Your fan base should know when you have specials. When you read interesting articles that will benefit them, you should share them with your fan base.

A fan club will help build a relationship between you and your customers.

We all know what it was like when we were kids and we had a favorite band or TV star. There is probably at least one performer that you sent a fan letter to. One performer you liked better than others. By joining their fan club, you became closer to the performer. You felt as if you knew them better. You had a vested interest in their success.

Years ago, I sent a fan letter to my favorite performer, and he sent me back a form letter and a picture. To this day I still have good feelings about Adam West as Batman.

What if there were a way to get your customers to do that sort of thing for you?

In the modern age it's not that difficult to build this fan base. And in an increasingly competitive marketplace, building that customer loyalty is more important than ever.

Here are some ideas:

First, get a Web site. I know everybody has a Web site, but not everybody has a Web site like yours. If you are not computer literate, don't be intimidated. Take a little bit of time to learn some software, and you can be up and running in no time.

Companies like godaddy.com, yahoo.com, mac.com, and others can provide you with the domain name, the easy-to-maneuver Web design software, and the storage space to have your site up and running.

Here's what you should have on your page:

- **An easy-to-remember domain name.**

It could be as simple as YourName.com or something that describes what it is you are selling. Make it catchy and simple.

> **It's important to remember that you form your fan club not to stroke your ego but to offer something more to your customers than your competition is offering.**

- **Important information that will benefit the client.**

For instance, the odds are that your customers have to buy a lot of goods and services in addition to what you are selling. They have a lot on their minds.

Don't waste their time. Have a Web presence that is easy to access and full of information that they can use. Don't just make it about your products, even though that is an equally important part of it. But have important information and helpful hints that can make your customers' lives easier.

- **Start writing a blog linked to your Web site.**

The blog can be a discussion around your observations about your industry. You can answer some frequently asked questions.

INFORMATION TO PUT ON YOUR WEB SITE

Link to interesting articles about changes in the industry. If you are selling to a business clientele, add links to important demographic information, sales trends, unique marketing ideas, or whatever else you can provide that will make your customers' jobs easier.

If your customer base is more consumer oriented, add links that apply to how your product or service will make their lives better. Have a page or two of references or comments from satisfied customers.

Include a gallery of pictures of these customers as well as their raves about the job you have done.

You can also tell a personal anecdote or two about your life to give the customer some insight as to who you are. All people are voyeurs. They like to know what other people are up to.

Don't be afraid to share some relevant personal issues. Remember, people will spend more money with people they feel they know and can trust. Make the comments relatable. Everybody can relate to a family getting a new puppy or having car problems or dealing with teenagers. No need to give them too much information. Just enough to let them connect to you and cast you in a positive light.

If you are going through a nasty divorce, it's probably best that you leave those details out. But don't be afraid to invite them into your life. After all, you know a lot about celebrities even though you've never met them. And if you know about these celebrities, you are more likely to consider spending your money on their latest CD or movie or watch their TV show.

People love to look in other people's medicine cabinets. We're nosy by nature. Don't be afraid to give your fan club a peek into your life.

• **Build a database.**

Form a fan club so you can send out e-mails to your customers when you have some really important news. Perhaps there's a special sale they can take advantage of or some fascinating information they can't live without.

Most Web software offers a contact program that allows your clients to sign up for a mailing list. Utilize this. Capture the addresses of your customers and prospects.

Then send them pertinent information when necessary. Don't load them up with junk e-mails, or your messages will go in the trash along with the spam for sexual enhancers and Nigerian banking schemes.

Let your fans know that when they hear from you, it's something important that will benefit them.

• **Uncover new leads.**

Offer some incentives for current customers who refer you to other potential clients. Make it easy for new potential customers to get in touch with you.

You could even have a way for Web surfers to ask you questions you could personally answer. Again, the more you can be a resource for your customer base, the bigger fans they will become.

You can also make the Web page interactive by having contests where they can only win prizes or discounts by visiting your site.

Be creative. Be ambitious. Visit other Web sites and steal the best ideas from them. It's important to remember that you form your fan club not to stroke your ego but to offer something more to your customers than your competition is offering.

The fan club reinforces your name and your awareness. The fan club becomes a part of the resources your customer uses to make smart buying decisions.

Obviously you will have to modify the Web page to fit your situation. If you are dealing with a business base, you will have different information than if you are dealing with a consumer-based clientele.

Keep the Web design crisp and clean. Keep it constantly updated with fresh information that makes your fans want to come back time and time again.

It would also be a good idea to get a page on a business networking site such as LinkedIn.com. Depending on what product you are selling, pages like MySpace or Facebook might be appropriate.

The more you can do to have the customer buy into the idea that you are part of their team, the more loyalty they will have to you and your product.

Not every practice has to be high tech to build the fan club. Some of the old tried-and-true methods to build a fan base still work incredibly well. Everybody loves free stuff. Offer your customers and potential customers usable promotional items. *Usable* being the operative word. Nobody needs more worthless junk like foam rubber penguins or some kind of snow globe paperweight. They only clutter up the desk.

But promotional items such as pens, coffee cups, notepads, and big-screen high definition television sets can be used and appreciated by everyone. Things like this will help maintain the fan base.

And you can never argue with the classics. Everybody loves it when you bring the staff donuts and bagels. But the ultimate way to build the fan base is through hard work and super customer service. Make sure that clients get everything they were promised and then some.

If there's a problem, resolve it right away. Don't ignore it and hope it will go away. Face it head on until the customer is satisfied.

Problems will happen. But if you make sure you take care of it right away, you will have a fan for life

☆

ACT TWO, SCENE SIX:

SAD SONGS
SAY SO MUCH*
*WITH ACKNOWLEDGMENT TO
ELTON JOHN AND BERNIE TAUPIN

When a singer sings a sad song—I mean really sings a sad song—it makes the audience feel their pain. It can make the audience feel sad.

When a comic tells a joke, it makes the audience laugh. A good joke can make the saddest person happy. It can completely change a person's attitude.

A suspenseful movie can make the audience afraid to sleep without a nightlight for months. A really good thriller will instill fear in people every time they open a closet door.

Every great performer manipulates emotions.

Manipulating emotions is not a bad thing. Indeed, in the world of sales it's a necessary thing. Have you ever been to a show and left feeling nothing? You probably have. Those are called bad shows. They bomb. The play closes on opening night. People leave the comedy club talking about how long the night seemed.

The same is true in sales. If you make a call and don't manipulate the emotions of the client, you are not going to get the sale. The customer will feel as if you have wasted his or her time. And you probably have.

To manipulate the emotions of your customer, the first thing you have to do is to manipulate your own emotions. Convince yourself you are going to make the sale. Have a positive attitude. Show off a good disposition. Walk into the meeting feeling the way you want the client to feel when it's all over.

A person who is in a bad mood can have that mood changed by hanging out with someone in a good mood. Conversely, a person in a good mood can have that changed by having coffee with a bitter, angry, sad curmudgeon. The dominant personality wins.

Go into that sales call with the dominant personality. Go into it with the attitude that you have what the customer wants and needs. Go into the performance with an attitude that you are going to close the sale.

Don't be cocky. Don't be arrogant. Be confident. Be comfortable. Be a firm believer in what you are about to achieve.

Every great performer manipulates emotions.

Comedians make people laugh. Singers help people fall in love. Movies can make people cry.

All are involuntary responses. All involve emotional manipulation. And the audiences wouldn't have it any other way.

ACT TWO, SCENE SEVEN:
STEAL FROM THE BEST

Every performer steals from other performers. Well, perhaps stealing is too strong a word. Let's say that performers are inspired, influenced, and educated by the great ones who came before them. And while stealing is too strong a word, stealing is really what they do.

The Rolling Stones stole from Muddy Waters. Mick Jagger stole his dance moves from Tina Turner. Countless other bands stole from the Rolling Stones. Eddie Murphy purloined from Richard Pryor. Johnny Carson loved Jack Benny and took many of his ideas. Yet they grabbed that inspiration and made it their own.

This idea seems so simple, but too many salespeople don't learn from the other salespeople in the field. The really successful salespeople have stolen ideas, styles, concepts, and tricks from those who went before them.

Don't be intimidated by the competition's success. Be inspired by it.

If the Beatles had been intimidated by Elvis, they wouldn't have been as big as they were. They saw what Elvis was doing and didn't mimic it, but they studied it and modified it to fit their style and their talents. They also stole from Buddy Holly, the Beach Boys, the bands they played with in Liverpool and Hamburg, and the music their parents listened to. All of those influences helped make them the most successful and dominant music force in the history of the industry.

Don't be jealous of a competitor's success. Find a way to make them jealous of yours. Use their own skills against them.

Don't be too proud to learn new ideas or relearn old ideas. By studying other salespeople and stealing—er, I mean, by being inspired by them—you might see something you used to do that you're not doing anymore. Look at what others are doing and take what will work for you and modify it to fit your style. You are never too old to learn. You are never too successful to learn.

So observe your competition. Ask questions. Take them out for drinks and ask them how they do it.

Everybody loves to talk about themselves. Don't be afraid to walk up to the best salespeople in your field and ask them how they do it. Talk to their customers and see what it is the customers like about their style.

Find out why people buy from the competition and modify those reasons to improve your own sales performance.

Now this cannot be stressed enough. When I say you should steal, I am not saying copy. No Elvis impersonator is as big as Elvis. You can't go far being a copy. You've got to be an original. You've got to be yourself. You've got to be unique.

You can be unique by being inspired by those in the same field. But you can't be unique if you just do what they do. You've got to do what they do, and then do it better in your own style.

And while I have been focusing on "borrowing" from others who are in the same line of sales as you are, you shouldn't limit yourself to being inspired only by others in the same field. Seek out successful salespeople in other fields. If you sell cars, see what successful real estate people are doing. If you sell advertising, learn from those who are selling insurance.

No Elvis impersonator is as big as Elvis. You can't go far being a copy.

Steal from the best. But don't be afraid to steal from the worst salespeople too. You can learn a lot by stealing from the really bad salespeople on the street. See what they are doing. And make sure you aren't doing it yourself.

We've all got bad habits. But until you see someone else with the same bad habit, you might not realize just how bad it is. If you look to the bad salespeople for inspiration, you can find it, if only to make yourself feel better about what you are doing.

In show business there really isn't anything new under the sun. Styles and technology may change, but a lot of the old tricks will still work today.

Recently Kanye West and 50 Cent, two rap stars, had a feud about whose CD would sell more. It got a lot of play in the press. People who weren't even into hiphop were talking about the competition. It helped generate a buzz and a buzz helps generate sales.

And while they may not admit this publicly, it really isn't any different than the rhubarb that Bob Hope and Bing Crosby used to have back in their heyday. Bob and Bing acted as if they were always in competition, and indeed they were. But their feud really benefited both of them. It gave people something to talk about.

When people are talking about you, it means they know who you are. And customers can't buy your product if they don't know who you are.

Stephen Colbert from Comedy Central announced he was running for President. If you were alive in the late '60s, you'll remember that Pat Paulsen, a comedian of the day, did the exact same thing with the exact same results. More publicity. More awareness. More sales.

Kanye and "Fitty" might have nothing in common with Bob and Bing on the surface, or for that matter Colbert with Paulsen, but they stole some old showbiz tricks to increase their market share.

There really aren't any new ideas out there. So go and steal some of the old ones. See what the salespeople of past generations did to make sales and polish it up for modern times.

They say that crime doesn't pay. But by stealing from those around you, both past and present, you can have a more successful career.

Observe.

Listen.

Learn.

Then go out and steal their customers.

Maybe crime does pay after all.

ACT THREE
Integrity, Appreciation, and Simplicity

☆

ACT THREE, SCENE ONE:
INTEGRITY IS JUST LIKE PORNOGRAPHY
Except You Can't Find It on the Internet

N ow might be an odd time to talk about integrity. After all, the last chapter was about stealing. But integrity is as important as talent and ability in both show business and in sales.

Historically in rock and roll there have always been the performers who were too high to perform. They would cancel dates. They would give a lackluster performance. They would only do a fraction of the time they were contracted to do. Their careers would have a quick burnout rate. If they didn't end up dead, they would end up finishing their careers as janitors.

If a Hollywood starlet was difficult on the set and wouldn't listen to her director, or be on time for her shoot, she would be replaced by another Hollywood starlet who would.

In show business and in the sales business, integrity is incredibly important. It's also a valued trait that probably can't be taught in a chapter of a book. But I'll try anyway. Integrity, much like pornography, is something you know when you see it. Unfortunately, we don't see as much integrity as we should.

If an actor gets the reputation for being pleasant to work with, professional, and always true to his word, he will get more jobs, better jobs, and higher paying jobs. An actor who is always on time for the shoot will save the producers a lot of money. An actress who works well with others makes the set a happier more productive workplace. Performers that work with the producers after the shoot to go on the talk shows and promote the product are more likely to be called for the next project. Actors who are true to their word are people you can depend on. And someone you can depend on is worth his or her weight in gold.

Think about your job.

Can your customers depend on you? Is your word your bond? Can you be trusted? Are you easy to work with? Do you work hard when it's expected? Give it your all every time? Do you deliver on the agreed date? Do you guarantee no surprises when the customer gets the bill?

Too many salespeople are always looking for the quick hit. They are looking for the easy way. Salespeople with integrity go the extra mile. They are honest with their customers even when they may be saying something they know the customer doesn't want to hear. They tell the client the truth even when it might mean they lose a sale or don't make as big a sale.

A salesperson who is not afraid to let customers know that they may not need every bell and whistle to fulfill their needs will be a salesperson that customers can count on when it's time to make future purchases.

Of course, you need the talent to make things happen. But without the integrity you will only sell the customer once. Without the integrity you will get a negative reputation. Without the integrity you will eventually fail.

Don't be like forgotten rock stars or spoiled actresses. Exceed expectations. Be honest. Be fair. Be reliable. It makes your success longer and more enjoyable.

☆

WITHOUT THE AUDIENCE,
It's Just Rehearsal

C an you imagine going to a rock concert and the singer starts off the show by telling the audience how he's doing? No! They always start off the show by saying or screaming a variation of "Hello, [insert name of city here]! How are you doing? Are you ready to rock?"

It's a cliche but the audience expects it.

Can you imagine going to a play in which the actors are more concerned about box office receipts than entertaining the audience?

It would seem like a no brainer, but it never ceases to surprise me how many times salespeople need to be reminded to make sure that every sales performance is about the client.

Too many times, a salesperson is more concerned about meeting quotas than about meeting the needs of the customer.

In show business, it's all about the audience, and in sales business it's always all about the customer. Everything else is inconsequential. It's all about the customer. It's all about the audience. No ifs, ands, or buts.

This can be difficult to remember sometimes because, in the real world of sales, you have to worry about quotas. You have to worry about sales managers, new product lines, budgets, expenses, and office politics.

But if you put all of the other worries on the back burner and only worry about your customers the way a performer worries about the audience, you'll be surprised how many of those other problems just go away.

Every successful entertainer has to worry about box office receipts, record sales, overhead, and the competition, just like a salesperson has to worry about inventory, budgets, paperwork, and their competition. But when it's showtime, you'd never know the performer has anything on their mind but the performance. When it's showtime, the entertainer only cares about making the audience happy.

Let your customers know how much you are concerned about them and their needs. Find out what your customers' needs, wants, and desires are. Show a genuine interest in them and then meet those needs.

Don't make it about you. Don't make it about the newest product line. Don't make it about you becoming salesperson of the month. Make it about them. Show interest in their needs. Ask questions to find out what those needs are. Show how what you have to offer will make them happier. How it will make their lives easier. Make them younger, healthier, prettier, richer, or wiser.

Every performer lives to make the audience happy. When the people pay their money to see a band, a play, a movie, a comic, or a dancing bear, they are there to have their needs met. They are not there to benefit the performers' needs. But here's the showbiz secret: If the audience members have their needs fulfilled, the performers' needs get met too.

There is a special name for entertainers who are more concerned about their needs than their audience's needs. It's called unemployed. They become an answer to a trivia question.

Make sure your audience gets what they came for and make sure they get more than they expected.

So how do you put all of the real world issues that involve you on the back burner and just focus on the customer? At the risk of sounding like an ad for a shoe company, "Just do it." When you meet with the client face-to-face, it is showtime. Nothing else matters. You are there for the customers to fulfill their needs. Even if they aren't sure yet what their needs are.

Forget about the fight you had with your spouse. Forget about the car problems that need to be addressed, or the pressure your boss is putting on you to make your sales. It's time to perform, and all that matters is you meeting your customers' needs.

If you watch late-night television, you have seen Jay, Dave, Conan, Jimmy, or Jon all working hard to make the audience laugh. They are all under intense pressure from the networks to deliver the largest audience in the target demographic. Their success in doing that results in bringing in millions of dollars in ad revenue.

These late-night hosts all have fights with their wives and girlfriends. They have car problems, kid issues, and the same life distractions everyone else has. But you'd never know it when the cameras are rolling. It's showtime. And when it's showtime, all that matters is the audience. All that matters is that the audience is having a good time.

And if the audience is having a good time, more people will tune in to the late-night shows. If more people tune them in, the pressure from the network to perform is less. Money issues become less of a problem because the hosts are making a lot of it. If the car breaks down, they can just buy a new one.

A lot of other problems go away or are diminished if you get up on that stage and make the customers' needs your needs.

These comics have also learned a very valuable lesson over the years. You see, not every audience is always there to have a good time. Especially in comedy there are times when the audience will not be in a mood to laugh. Just like there are clients who are not in a mood to buy.

Learn some of the tricks comedians use. Comedians will throw out some of their best material at the beginning to do two things. They will obviously want the audience to laugh. But they are also sizing up the room. They are listening and observing to get a feel for what kind of material the audience is looking for.

Are they looking for clean or dirty jokes? Are they interested in long stories or quick punch lines? If the comedian gets off script and starts to talk to the audience, will the audience get out of hand?

These are all things that comedians size up from watching the audience. They begin by observing the audience when they walk into the club or theater. They pay close attention to whether the audience laughs at their jokes and also how the audience members are listening to the jokes.

Isn't it the same on a sales call?

When you meet a customer face-to-face for the first time, you should have already sized up the situation by observing the surroundings. Notice the customer's body language. See how the customer is responding and react accordingly.

Hit them with some of your "A" material early to intrigue them and command their attention. Don't waste their time. Notice how they are responding to your presentation and then adapt accordingly.

So remember when it's time to meet with the customer, you are not there to reach your sales quota. You are not there to win some sales contest. You are not there to get your boss off your back.

When you see that customer, the lights are on, the curtain is up, it's showtime. You are there to deliver to the audience. And when you deliver to the audience, a lot of the other problems all go away.

☆

ACT THREE, SCENE THREE:
A QUICK RANDOM THOUGHT
Less Really Can Be More

How many times have you seen a movie preview and thought, "This is going to be a great movie"? But how many times has it really been a great movie?

You arrive at the theater with great anticipation because you had seen the coming attractions for the film the last time you went to the multiplex. The coming attractions made you laugh. They gave you an adrenaline rush. They made you feel good about what you were about to see. The coming attractions made you happy to part with your money.

You settle in with a five-gallon diet drink and enough popcorn to feed a Third World nation. The movie begins and you soon find out that all the good parts were in the preview.

You feel your attitude shift as you slowly realize that the rest of the movie sucks.

You had walked into the movie theater where you anticipated viewing the next *Gone with the Wind* only to walk out feeling as if you had just seen *Porkies 12*. How did you feel? Ripped off? Did you want your $9.50 back? Did you bad-mouth the movie to your friends? Did you vow to never go see another film with the same stars? Maybe you vowed never to go to the movies again.

Take a lesson from some of the smaller films and lower your expectations.

Obviously you have to promote your product or service. But how do you do it without overselling? You have to motivate people to buy what you're selling the same way the movie preview has to motivate people to come to the theater. You have to put your best foot forward. You have to sell the sizzle.

But make sure there is plenty of substance after the sizzle.

Hype can be one of your greatest friends and one of your biggest enemies. You need to create some hype about your product line to build excitement. You need to hype your goods and services to be noticed, to generate interest, and to generate sales.

Anybody can sell somebody something once with enough hype. Here's the problem. If all you have is the hype, that's the only time you'll make the sale. You'll never get the repeat business. And you need the repeat business and the word of mouth to make the big bucks.

Take a lesson from some of the smaller films and lower your expectations. Every year a couple of movies with smaller budgets and no big-name stars come on the scene and thoroughly surprise the public. The previews are enough to get a few people in the theaters but not enough to create a huge opening-day box office.

Moviegoers come into the theater with no major expectations, but when they leave, they are pleasantly surprised. Instead of feeling as if somebody just stole their money from them, they go spread the word among their friends.

Unless you are a door-to-door salesman selling steak knives, you need the return sales and you need the referrals. You won't get them if, like the movie preview, you put all of your good stuff up front and don't back it up. You need to provide stellar service. You need to back it up with a product that does more than you said it would.

You should always over deliver.

So take a lesson from the movie industry's coming attractions: Don't oversell. By having the buyers pleasantly surprised by what happens after they buy, it will help to guarantee that there will be favorable word of mouth about you on the streets. By lowering expectations and increasing results, you will help to guarantee that there will be a sequel— if you know what I mean.

ACT THREE, SCENE FOUR:
USING PROPS
(or If It Works for Carrot Top, It Can Work for You)

The next time you watch a movie or a TV show, pay attention to how the characters use props to further the plot. In any theatrical production the propmaster is one of the most important members of the crew. No prop is ever put on stage or in a scene without a purpose.

Are you using props in your sales performance?

Depending on what you are selling, you can use a million different props to help further your sales message. Some of the obvious props would be samples of your products. Perhaps a PowerPoint presentation might be a prop that you can use. It could be as simple as a piece of paper with references from some satisfied customers.

In a sales performance you are going to need props. The question is what props do you need and how should you use them?

I knew a woman in sales who was having a tough time seeing a difficult client. This client was a busy man, but he had a lot of money to spend. It was easy for him to keep saying no when she tried to set up an appointment. In fact most times he never said no to her. His secretary did. The customer saw no benefit in seeing this salesperson.

So one day she got a little creative. She took a shoebox and made a three-sided cut in the middle of it to make it look like a door. She got out some colored markers and construction paper to make it look like this was a door to his office. She even put a small sign on the door with his name on it.

Then she bought a pair of toddler-sized tennis shoes. She took one of those shoes and glued it to the bottom of the shoe box halfway through the cut in the box. She then took it to a florist where she ordered a nice plant and had them deliver the plant and the shoebox and the shoe with a note that said, "Tell me what I need to do to get my foot in the door."

I might also mention that this project was very well done. She was a woman who loved doing crafts. Had this been slipshod, it may have come across as some sort of a ransom note or a third-grade art project.

It might have been considered a little hokey. It was also a little risky. But since she wasn't getting the appointment anyway, she had nothing to lose.

As I'm sure you've figured out by now, she got the appointment and the sale. After all, I wouldn't have mentioned this if it had failed. She used a prop to get what she wanted. She used a prop to further the plot.

This prop fit her personality. Yet an idea like this might not work for you, which is why you need to think of props that you can use that fit your style.

Be creative. Brainstorm with your manager and your coworkers. Come up with unique ideas that will stand out yet not detract from your message. The wrong prop at the wrong time can be distracting. For instance, the light sabres in *Star Wars* were great for the fight scenes in that movie but would have been totally out of place if used by Leonardo DiCaprio and Kate Winslet on the *Titanic*.

If Leo and Kate had used the light sabres, the audience would have been stunned. The prop would have been totally ineffective, and the actors would have completely lost the audience.

The right prop at the right time helps you make the sale. The wrong prop will distract the client, you'll lose your momentum, and you'll probably lose the sale.

To determine the right prop, ask yourself the following questions:

- What am I trying to accomplish by using this prop?
- Am I trying to set an appointment?
- Am I trying to educate the client on the benefits of my product?
- Am I trying to reinforce a point I've made?

- Am I trying to close the sale?
- Am I trying to maintain a front-of-mind awareness and a positive image with the client?

How many props you should use and when you should use them really depends on your personality and what you are selling.

As an example, think of a stand-up comic. Many comics get their point across without using many props. Comics like Carrot Top, Gallagher, and Rip Taylor wouldn't have an act if it weren't for props. Make it fit your style.

Find out what works best for you and do it.

The wrong prop at the wrong time can be distracting.

Here are some idea starters to answer the questions just asked. These are by no means the definitive answers but just some thoughts to get you thinking. There are a million more ideas that can be used. Think of some yourself.

Am I trying to set an appointment?

I've mentioned the foot-in-the-door idea. But your prop doesn't have to be that elaborate. It could be as simple as sending a letter. You could also send a plant, a sample of your product, or some donuts. Do something memorable that your competition isn't doing.

Try to avoid the worthless specialty trinkets. Does anyone really need another stress ball? If you are using a specialty item, make it something clients can use such as pens, mouse pads, or fishing boats.

Am I trying to further the sales process along?

You'll use different props for this. You'll use props such as testimonial letters, photographs of people using your product, a sample of the product, or anything that would make the customer comfortable about buying your goods or services.

Depending on the type of presentation you are making, you could be implementing a PowerPoint display or some other technological device to help sell your ideas.

Remember, the props are to be used to support the message you are delivering, not to distract from it. The prop should support your message and not be so overpowering that it becomes your message.

Am I trying to reinforce a point I've made?

A demonstration of the product, a video of satisfied customers, or a copy of newspaper or magazine articles might be the props you would use here.

Know your clients. Know your product. Know what works for you. You have to use the props that you feel comfortable with. These props would fit your personality and your product or service.

Be creative. Be unique. Be yourself. Use your props effectively and the force will be with you.

GIVE AT THE OFFICE
and Have the Office Give Back to You

"If you haven't got any charity in your hoart, you havo tho worst klnd of heart trouble."

—Bob Hope

They say it is better to give than to receive, and many generous stars and celebrities have found that to be the case. Most of the biggest performers have special causes. You see them on the red carpet going to charity events for cancer, AIDS, hungry children, and the heartbreak of psoriasis.

But the question is this: Are they helping humanity or helping themselves?

The answer is they're doing both.

By getting involved in various charities and social work, they not only are trying to make the world a better place, they are making themselves more marketable.

Take, for example, the Muscular Dystrophy Association (MDA) and Jerry Lewis. Jerry Lewis was one of the biggest stars of the 1950s when he and Dean Martin were tearing up the silver screen and the nightclub circuit. Anyone under the age of 60 might not realize just how big a star Jerry Lewis was.

But it's his work with the Muscular Dystrophy Association every year that keeps him in the nation's front-of-mind awareness every year. By working the telethon, Jerry remains a contemporary figure and not just a fond memory in the old folks home.

Every Labor Day for more than 40 years Jerry has been raising millions of dollars while raising his public image. The telethon not only benefits the image of Jerry Lewis, it benefits all the performers he brings out on stage, many of whom haven't been on TV for decades. These artists get time before a national audience, which means more jobs for them the rest of the year.

Both the entertainers and seriously ill kids benefit from Jerry Lewis and his involvement in the MDA.

It doesn't take a rocket scientist to figure out how being involved in various charities and community events will benefit the sales superstar. By getting involved and by going to fund-raising events, you will network, build a positive public image, and benefit others as well as yourself. By being involved in charity work, you will meet prospective customers. You will meet people who will refer you to prospective customers. You will generate sales, and you will have the opportunity to make the world a little bit better.

The best way to get involved is to find a cause in which you have a personal interest. Unfortunately, almost everyone has been touched by a devastating disease. These diseases all have fund raisers that you can attend.

Perhaps your interest lies with children's issues. Or church events. Or community sporting events. A real estate agent I know started out as a one-person shop 15 years ago. His advertising budget was limited, so he focused on sponsoring Little League teams. His strategy was that he would build goodwill with the parents of those kids. And sooner or later the parents of those kids were going to buy or sell a house.

The concept worked.

As his sales grew, so did his sponsorship of kids' activities. Baseball, football, volleyball, and soccer teams all over town wore uniforms with his name on the back. Occasionally he would write a check to some youth athletic organization to buy equipment or maintain a playing field. These donations often made it on the evening news. He'd be on TV or in the paper holding a big check helping the children in town.

You can't buy that kind of publicity. And the goodwill he was building translated into more sales.

**It doesn't take a rocket scientist
to figure out how being involved
in various charities and community
events will benefit the sales superstar.**

Soon his little one-man shop had hundreds of agents working for him. He had offices all over town. And while his charity work alone didn't build that business, it was accountable for a large part of the awareness of his agency. The networking he did while working with children's athletics generated sales, while building the foundation for future generations of customers.

So get involved. Find a cause. Help make your city a better place.

It's a definite win-win situation.

☆

THE TABLOIDS
Didn't Get Rich Because People Didn't Care

We're all voyeurs. We don't want to admit it. We'll deny it if confronted with it, but we are all voyeurs. Whether you are watching reality TV, reading the tabloids, or checking out what's in the other shoppers' shopping carts, we all want to know what other people are up to.

Which is why successful showbiz salespeople will allow themselves to be the "voyee."

No matter what kind of work you are in, your customers, your fellow workers, all want to know more about you. Just as the customers of movies, TV shows, and CDs all want to know more about the artists. That's why you've got to let them peek behind the curtain.

Let them get a little insight into you. Insight that they think only they have. Let them know something memorable about you and your personal life to make a lasting imprint.

The difficult part is deciding what you want them to know. For instance, if you've got a wife and two kids that's great. But so does everybody else. What differentiates you from everyone else? What stories can you tell that will make the audience smile and remember you?

I had a former general manager who was divorced. Now unfortunately in the radio business it's not that unusual to be divorced. But instead of telling stories about her ex, she told stories about the "plaintiff."

To be honest with you I'm not even sure if most of the stories were true. But she told them with a sense of humor in a way that would make her stand out from any other divorcee. Even if people didn't remember her name at first, they always remember that at one time she was married to the "plaintiff." It was two years before I even knew that "plaintiff" had a real name.

When you tell a story about yourself, don't be bragging. Don't talk about how you are the leading salesperson in the region. Don't talk about the brand new expensive sports car you drive.

Tell a story about a human foible. Tell a story that makes you relatable. Tell a story that could have happened to the person hearing the story. For example, talk about the difficulties you had finding a plumber. Talk about how you burned yourself last weekend grilling a steak. Talk about the everyday (yet not mundane or boring) aspects of everyday life that you are going through.

If you did the stand up routine, community play, or karaoke that I mentioned in an earlier chapter, these would be the sorts of things that you would mention.

By letting people be a "voyee" into your life, you are helping to build your image. More than just the clothes you wear or the car you drive, you are now letting them see a little bit into your life. You are making yourself more memorable.

And people can't buy from you if they don't remember who you are.

Don't make it a story where they'll feel bad about you. Make it an uplifting tale. Make it a story that will make them laugh.

Now you might ask yourself why you should do something like this. Why? Because we are all voyeurs. We all want to look inside the medicine cabinet. We all want to get a peek at the performer's life behind the scenes.

Make your story memorable, relatable, positive, and brief. And make sure you show some interest in your client's story too.

Make it a two-way street so that you know more about your customer. The more you know, the more you'll be able to relate and to serve their needs.

ACT THREE, SCENE SEVEN:

THE "R" WORD

"Some actors couldn't figure out how
to withstand the constant rejection.
They couldn't see the light at the end of
the tunnel."

—Actor Harrison Ford

It's been said that you are not truly in show business, or for
that matter truly in sales, until you have heard a variation of
the phrase, "Thanks, but no thanks," at least a thousand times.

Rejection is part of the game.

In your mind you know that hearing the word *no* is just part
of the game. You can rationalize and reconcile the fact that
rejection is just part of doing your job. It's an occupational
hazard. In your cognitive moments, you realize that you can't
close every deal just as every actor can't land every part they
audition for.

Of course, the cognitive doesn't always jibe with the emotional.

While some people may disagree, actors, musicians, and salespeople really are human. And being human they are going to be depressed and disappointed when they get turned down. Nobody likes to be told no. Nobody likes to feel that they weren't good enough. Especially when they really wanted the part they were auditioning for, or really wanted to close that sale.

It's hard when an actor knows that he or she is perfect for a part. It's hard when a salesperson knows that the company's goods or services are perfect for the client. Still they don't close the deal.

It's a sad fact of life that you can do your best and still not achieve what you set out to accomplish.

So how do you deal with rejection and not have it cripple you or affect you on your next call?

Become schizophrenic.

Not literally but figuratively. By becoming schizophrenic I mean develop two personalities. Become a person and a product.

The person is obviously who you are when you are hanging out with your family and friends. The person is who you are and what you do when you are not selling. The customer is not rejecting you as a person.

By becoming a product, you can detach yourself from your feelings and look at things in a more objective manner.

By becoming a product when a customer says no, you can understand that they are not saying no to you as a person, but rather they are saying no to you as a product—just as a customer might choose Coke over Pepsi or Miller over Bud. Just because a customer chose one over the other doesn't mean that the other is bad. They could only pick one and unfortunately you weren't it.

The customer's rejection doesn't reflect on you and your self-worth.

There are a lot of choices out there and you are not going to be right for everyone or, more specifically, right for everyone every time.

"If you're a car salesman, and someone says, 'This is a terrible car, I'm not buying it,' it doesn't mean they hate you. They just don't like your product. I think that's a mistake a lot of people in show business make ... they're so tied to their act they take everything personally."
—TV Talk Show Host Jay Leno

It would be virtually impossible to list every time an actor or a performer was turned down at one audition and then called weeks, months, or years later by the casting director to be hired for another role.

In show business, just as in business in general, sometimes timing is everything. Not every rejection is forever.

The key is to always make a good impression when you are on a sales call. The customer may not want what you have now, but six months from now what you are selling might be just what they need. If your sales performance was memorable, by keeping in contact with the customers, you will help insure that you are always in their minds when they think of what you are selling.

Analyze what went wrong.

Don't beat yourself up, but ask yourself what you could have done better. Ask yourself if there was something that you could have done that might have made a difference.

Entertainers are constantly reviewing themselves and watching tapes of their performances to see what they can do better. Not enough salespeople do that. And they need to.

Put a mini-recorder in your coat pocket or purse to record the sales call. Then listen to the presentation when you are alone. Be honest with yourself and replay the whole sales process and see if there was a place where you could have done something different.

Don't be afraid to go back to the customer and ask if there was something you could have done. See if there was something you didn't explain properly to make the sale.

When John Ratzenberger, better known as Cliff in *Cheers*, did his initial audition, he failed miserably. But as he was leaving, he asked the producers if they had a part for a bar know-it-all. He then went on to audition as Cliff and started talking about the origin of the office furniture. He didn't make the initial sale. But he went back with another idea and it worked.

Don't go back to the customer with an attitude or in a confrontational mode, but go back on more of a fact-finding mission. People love to give their opinions. You'd be surprised what they might say.

Just as every audience member loves to give a review of any movie, play, or concert they've seen, your customer will more than likely be happy to give you a review of your performance. Thank them for their honest appraisal and do your best to give them what they want.

> Chaplin was a man of few words when he was on the silver screen. But he was a man who knew what he was saying when he wrote those immortal words, "Smile though your heart is breaking."

Have plenty of outside interests.

Even though it's important that you eat, drink, and sleep the sales business, it's just as important that you have plenty of other passions. Have something to take your mind off work. Rejection is easier to take when you go home at night if you have to coach your child's Little League game, attend a class in photography, or sell antique dolls on eBay.

It's also amazing how many times a good idea might pop into your head about work when you are focusing on something completely different.

If after a bad day you go to a bar, or just sit home and stew about it, you will only get more depressed, and it won't benefit you at all. But if your mind is relaxed and on some other interest, you'll be amazed at how many times a great idea will pop into your head that will help you bounce back tomorrow.

While being a success in sales will put food on your table, man does not live by bread alone. Make sure that you have plenty of other interests to keep you refreshed and relaxed.

Charlie Chaplin was a man of few words when he was on the silver screen. But he was a man who knew what he was saying when he wrote those immortal words, "Smile though your heart is breaking."

Those are great words to live by. Just as we've pointed out that you should never let them see you sweat, you should never let them see that you are hurt by rejection. Smile though your heart is breaking and not only will the people around you believe that everything is fine, you'll start to believe it too.

And when you believe everything is fine, you'll dust yourself off and get back up on that sales stage.

THE FINALE

"And in the end ... the love you make is equal to the love you take."

—The Beatles

The finale in a more traditional sales setting would be called the close. The finale occurs after you have started with an attention grabber, told the story, and now you are going to make it all come together with a big finish.

Now is the time to really sell it.

If your sales performance were a Broadway musical, the close is the big production number that has them dancing in the aisle. If your sales performance were a stand-up routine, the close is the big punchline. If your sales performance were a drama, the close is when the good guys capture the murderer.

My point is this: Everything you have done prior to this leads up to the close.

Too many salespeople are timid when it comes to the finale. They are afraid to ask for the order. They don't deliver the close with any pizzazz. If you've done everything else right, the customer is waiting for the big finish.

People like to buy. Make your close something memorable. Make it big.

Have you ever been to a movie and when you left the theater you weren't sure about the ending? You were puzzled and unsatisfied. You felt as if you'd wasted the last two hours of your life.

Don't leave your customer feeling the same way by ending with a soft finish. When it's time for the finale, make sure you leave no doubt it's time for the payoff. Don't bury it. Don't be hesitant or unsure of yourself.

If you're a veteran, don't be too comfortable or too blasé with the close either. People like to buy. Make your close something memorable. Make it big. Give it all you've got.

Many times the finale is the only thing the audience will talk about as they leave the theater.

Make sure when you give your big finish that you give it with style. You give it with confidence. Give it in a way that will get your audience to give you a standing ovation.

And in sales you get the standing ovation when the customer makes the buy.

ENCORE

"Take a bow."
—TV Variety Show Host Ed Sullivan

There you are at a great concert. The band finishes. And they just walk off the stage never to be seen again.

What kind of a letdown would it be if the band didn't come back and do at least one encore? Even if you really enjoyed the show, you'd leave the theater complaining and grumbling.

You paid your money. You gave the entertainer your time. Assuming it was a great performance, you expect an encore.

Now think of how that applies to a salesperson.

Do you know how many salespeople never make a return appearance after they have closed the sale? Far too many. After making a sale, too many salespeople are concentrating on the next performance and not enough are concentrating on their encore.

It's as if they are on the bus driving to the next town before the house lights go up.

A salesperson should always make an appearance after the sale, if only to see how the product or service is working. Or to see if the customer has any problems or questions. Or to get a referral from the client.

Too many times salespeople will not follow up after they have closed the deal. Why? Are they ashamed of what they sold? Do they think it's not important? Are they lazy?

The encore is the easy part of the show. You have already got the customers in the palm of your hand. Now all you are doing is basking in the glow and giving the audience more of what they want.

> **A salesperson should always make an appearance after the sale, if only to see how the product or service is working. Or to see if the customer has any problems or questions. Or to get a referral from the client.**

Often the encore is the part of the show the audience really remembers. It's the feeling the audience has when they leave the auditorium. It's the feeling they remember when the performer comes through town again next year and asks you to buy another ticket.

So go back. Take a bow. Do an encore.

Visit the customer for service after the sale. Make sure the customers are happy. Fix any problems they may have. Let them know that you weren't just taking their money and running.

Don't forget the encore. It will help guarantee that after your performance your customer will be singing a happy tune.

MAKE IT A
LONG-RUNNING
ENGAGEMENT

"If you ask what is the single most important key to longevity, I would have to say it is avoiding worry, stress, and tension. And if you didn't ask me, I'd still have to say it."
—The Legendary George Burns

The other day I was talking to a friend of mine. He's 80 years old and a jazz drummer. As we sat, he told me of the old days when he was playing with the Count Basie Orchestra. He was telling me what Ella Fitzgerald was like.

He told stories of being a black man playing white clubs in the '50s and '60s. He talked about the gigs he played last week and the jobs he had lined up for the months to come.

Here he was, still going strong at 80 years old.

A ton of performers have continued to be successful way past their so-called youth-oriented prime. George Burns, Bob Hope, Frank Sinatra, and Rodney Dangerfield immediately come to mind as performers who adapted and were relevant to audiences well into their 80s.

How many stars are still going strong even though they've reached retirement age? Paul McCartney, the Rolling Stones, Bob Dylan, and more are still packing concert halls and auditoriums even though they don't need the money, and they could be taking it easy.

But when you love what you do and you can make others happy by doing it, why would you quit? Especially when what you do will keep you rolling in the green stuff.

So as America gets older, what can we learn from the performers who are still relevant well into their golden years?

First let's differentiate between the classics and the nostalgia acts. There is a big difference in both the perception of the audience and pay scale they receive. The nostalgia acts are the bands that get on stage and sing old songs and try to relive the "good old days." These bands will play county fairs, casino lounges, and kids' birthday parties. They will have to work 10 times harder than the classic acts and still make a third as much money.

These acts have never evolved. They got caught in a time warp. They found a little success and were happy with it and never progressed. You can make a living as a nostalgia act but wouldn't you rather be a headliner? A star? A classic?

The classic acts are the acts that still seem fresh even after they have been doing it for generations. Take Rodney Dangerfield. Please. Rodney was in his 60s and 70s and still a major draw with young audiences. He never gave the impression he was some old guy trying to relate to younger audiences. He was just Rodney.

David Letterman is another great example. He stays relevant to a modern audience even after almost 30 years in television by constantly adding new ideas to the program. Even old ideas like the top 10 list stay fresh because the topics are current, and he sells it every night like it's the first time.

Now whether it's because they love what they do, or they haven't saved enough for retirement, more and more baby boomers are going to work into their golden years. But how do they avoid being a nostalgia act and make the big bucks as a classic act?

In sales a nostalgia act would be someone who keeps calling on the same clients that they've been seeing for years. They don't present new ideas. They don't prospect new accounts. Yet they make a living because they know that good ol' Charley will always buy something from them.

The classic acts go out on tour when they have a new product to promote. When Springsteen goes on tour, he has a new CD. He gives his audiences something fresh as well as the old stuff that the fans want to hear.

To avoid being a nostalgia act, you should have a young attitude. That doesn't mean you stay out all night clubbing like some young Hollywood starlet. It doesn't mean you wear trendy clothes that are not appropriate for someone your age. It means that you stay on top of all the latest trends and changes.

You've seen it around the office. A salesperson hits a certain age and starts to just go through the motions. They don't study new product lines. They are reluctant to adopt new systems. New technology is easier to be bitched about than to learn.

These salespeople are one step from being Willy Loman in *Death of a Salesman*. What an awful way to live your life. Change is inevitable. Embrace it.

If I may go back to using Rodney Dangerfield as an example, when comedy exploded on cable TV, Rodney could have sat around with some of his old cronies and talked about how things were so much better in the old days. He could have talked about when Lenny Bruce was around and how they opened for strippers in smoky dive bars.

He could have sat back and reminisced about how he liked working the *Ed Sullivan Show* and *The Tonight Show* because they had such a large national audience, instead of the relatively small audience HBO was bringing at the time.

But instead of bitching about what used to be, Rodney Dangerfield stepped up to the plate, embraced the new technology, and hit it out of the park. He came up with a series of young comedian specials through which he reached a younger, hipper demographic.

He took the new technology and the changes in his industry in stride and used them to benefit his needs.

A lot of his contemporaries decided to just sit around and complain that things have changed. These are the guys you don't remember.

What about you and your industry?

Even if you are years away from reaching 60, you'd better start thinking about how you are going to react and adapt to the changes. Today they are coming at you at a faster pace than ever before. which means that you could be a dinosaur in your industry at an earlier age than ever before if you don't keep on top of what is going on.

Be one step ahead of the competition and really prosper.

Be thinking outside the box and be ready for new ideas— ideas like the ones that I am proposing here to keep ahead of the competition.

Don't be a nostalgia act, getting the same old orders from the same tired customers. Be like Rodney Dangerfield and keep mining for a new audience. Keep looking for a way to increase your market share.

Keep current. Adapt. And challenge yourself to be better. If you do, you'll be able to continue to be a superstar long after others have faded away.

INDEX

Willis, Bruce, 11
Winfrey, Oprah, 49, 50, 51, 52
Winslet, Kate, 97
write jokes, 41
wrong props, 97

Z

Zellweger, Renee, 11

ABOUT THE AUTHOR

T om Becka is a successful stand-up comic, radio talk
   show host, salesman, sales manager, teacher, author, and
motivational speaker

As a comic he has opened for the likes of Jerry Seinfeld,
Sam Kinison, Darrell Hammond, the rock band Chicago, and
jazz great George Benson.

His opinions about everything from presidential politics to
great restaurants have been heard on the *NBC Nightly News*,
Oprah, *48 Hours*, *Nightline*, *MSNBC*, *C-SPAN*, and *CNBC*.

He has sold advertising, electronics, fertilizer, and clothing.
In high school he was recognized for selling more apple pies
than any other employee at the fast food restaurant where he

worked. He has taken all of these skills and life experiences to create a new way to make bad salespeople good, good salespeople great, and great salespeople incredible.

Once you've read *There's No Business Without the Show*, you'll never go on another traditional sales call again.

☆

ENTERTAIN, INFORM
AND ENERGIZE
YOUR SALES STAFF!

Want to learn more about
There's No Business Without the Show
in a personal and entertaining way?

Invite Tom Becka to speak to your convention, meeting, or sales force. His unique message and lively delivery will inspire and motivate your staff or sales team to reach new heights.

For more information, references and availability, visit *www.TomBecka.com*.

ORDER COPIES FOR
YOUR SALES STAFF!

Customer Name: _____

Date: _____

Shipping Address: _____

City: _____ State: _____ Zip: _____

Telephone: (___) _____

Email: _____

Hardcover = $21.95 x _____(number of copies) $ _____

Paperback = $18.95 x _____(number of copies) $ _____

Sales Tax (7% when shipped to Nebraska addresses only) $ _____

Shipping & Handling (allow 2 weeks)

Shipping Costs: $3.00 for 1ˢᵗ book

                    $1.50 for each additional book $ _____

                            TOTAL $ _____

PAYMENT METHOD

☐ Check enclosed made payable to "Orpheum Brothers Press"

☐ VISA   ☐ MasterCard   ☐ American Express   ☐ Discover

Name on Card: _____

Billing Address (if different from above) _____

Account Number: _____

CVV_____ Exp. Date_____

(3 digits on back of card near signature on Visa/MC/Discover - 4 digits on front of AmEx)

Cardholder's Signature: _____

Mail This Form to:
Orpheum Brothers Press • P.O. Box 31267
Omaha, Nebraska 68131
www.TomBecka.com

THERE*S NO
BUSINESS
WITHOUT THE
SH☆W!

PLACING YOUR ORDER

MAIL this form to:
Orpheum Brothers Press.
P. O. Box 31267
Omaha, Nebraska 68131

FAX order form to:
(413) 669-8870

EMAIL your order to:
orders@conciergemarketing.com

ONLINE orders may be placed at:
www.TomBecka.com

THANK YOU!